Tears of Silence

Photographs by Donna Moyseuik
Editorial Consultants: Linda Macdonald,
Margaret Ordway, Daniel Macdonald
and Flavio Belli

Tears of Silence

Jean Vanier

Darton, Longman & Todd
London

First published in Great Britain in 1973 by
Darton, Longman & Todd Limited
85 Gloucester Road, London SW7 4SU
© Jean Vanier 1970
Typeset by Cranmer Brown (Filmsetters) Ltd
Printed in Great Britain by
Fletcher & Son Ltd, Norwich
ISBN 0 232 51188 8

FOREWORD

by

Therese Vanier

Born in 1928, Jean Vanier was educated in England and Canada. In 1942 he entered the Royal Naval College, Dartmouth and went to sea in 1945. After some years in the Royal Navy and Royal Canadian Navy, he resigned and gave up a naval career in favour of studying philosophy. While pursuing these studies he lived and worked in a community for students outside Paris. He obtained his doctorate in philosophy in 1963 and seemed about to embark on a university teaching career in Canada. However, about this time he became aware of the circumstances and needs of mentally handicapped adults living in French psychiatric hospitals and in 1964 he moved in to a rather dilapidated house in the village of Trosly-Breuil north east of Paris, with one or two helpers and four mentally handicapped men. They repaired and added to the house which they called "L'ARCHE". This name came eventually to be used for the organisation as a whole. Eight years after this small beginning, there are 120 mentally handicapped men and women living in the original and neighbouring villages, forming with the assistants a community which numbers over 200 people. In France the next community, "La Merci," started in a large abandoned farm near Cognac and the third, "Les Trois Fontaines," is near Boulogne sur mer. Meanwhile "Daybreak" had opened near Toronto in Canada and Asha Niketan (Home of Hope) in Bangalore, India. The first ARCHE community in England hopes to open a house near Canterbury early in 1973.

In England a recent Government White Paper has highlighted the need to provide suitable accommodation for those at present housed in sub-normality hospitals and who do not in fact need residential medical care. "L'ARCHE" will join its efforts to those of other voluntary organisations and local authorities already helping to care for such people in small groups living in a protected environment. It will bring the particular stamp of Jean Vanier's work with handicapped people: a great sense of the primacy of the individual over such elements as productivity, efficiency and success. A respect and love for the weak ones of society precisely because they *are* weak and can thus contribute something essential to the very society which tends to reject them. Jean Vanier often says that where handicapped people are present "things tend to happen". The spontaneous warmth and sincerity of their greeting, the lack of self consciousness, the joy in very simple things, their sensitivity to and concern for others, their direct and generous attitude to prayer and worship, all help to break down barriers in and between "normal people".

In the ARCHE communities assistants and handicapped live in family size groups, sharing all aspects of daily life: meals, work, recreation, hobbies, fiestas, and often long trips and pilgrimages.

Just as young children may do, handicapped people have the capacity to touch the hearts of others. If a "normal person" approaches one who is in some sense weak and in need of help and in so doing the weak member feels that he is loved and wanted, a new desire to live is born in him. He may respond in some hardly perceptible way to the one who brings him this life, it may be a smile, or a brightening of the eyes or a serenity previously unknown, but this starts a healing process in the "assistant" who may realise for the first time the extraordinary power he has to "make life worth living". Thus a whole process of mutual healing is born and spreads out beyond the immediate situation. The anxieties, depression, crises of the handicapped are gradually stilled, and his capacity to teach values which much of western society is losing sight of, revealed.

When John Vanier moved in to "L'ARCHE" with mentally handicapped friends, he was much criticized by those who said he was abandoning a career which would give him the opportunity to use the already marked influence he had on young people. What has happened, of course, is that living his religious and philosophical beliefs has allowed an infinitely greater attraction for the young who will not tolerate a dichotomy between belief, teaching and practice. The assistants in the Arche Communities are mainly young school or university leavers and young men and women are asking to come to work and live with the handicapped in increasing numbers. They find a school of life which may not be easy, but which strikes them as valid and valuable and in which undoubtedly they renew hope, joy and often faith, finding a sense of purpose and vocation. They come for short or long periods, some with professional training which they can put to good use, others seek some form of training at a later date to allow them to return and give more "professional" help. By the time they do this, however, they know that the important aspect of life with the handicapped is not just professionalism but a capacity to listen and respond to the Tears of Silence of the rejected and weak. So that the weak may heal the strong, and those who think themselves strong, the weak.

The publisher told me this layout would be mistaken for poetry and severely criticised as bad poetry or no poetry. I said, fine, I don't care what people say about the style for this was never meant to be poetry. I am only trying to open people's hearts to the wounded and the rejected. They are the ones that are important.

JV

Our lives are fleeting moments in which are found the seeds of eternal peace, unity and love as well as the seeds of war, dissension and indifference. When will we rise and awaken to the choice before each of us, to water and to give light to one or the other of these two seeds?
Must we accept damnation or can humanity be saved?

This book is dedicated to all those of the House of the Dying in Calcutta. It is dedicated to the faces that are shown here, faces and people who represent you and me, and all those who are fearful, and all those who aspire to universal brotherhood.

I grieve to speak of love and yet not love as I should.
I ask forgiveness of the many I have wounded
and of the many I have passed without seeing their wounds.
Pray for me, my brother.

How many times
      a meeting has struck barriers
            cement blocks
                  in me
heart of stone
heart of stone
      unable to listen
         i fear
         and fly by
who can liberate me from myself?

he who clutches desperately to security —

to every day habits, work, organization, friends,
family . . . . .

closed off . . . .

no longer lives:

more than security,

life needs

adventure

risk

dynamic activity

self-giving

presence to others

in the paths of our existence

      there are at times obstacles . . . . . .

           rocks barring the road . . . . . .

if these obstacles appear too great

      or if we, through fatigue or other reasons,

        are deflated,

        then we sit and weep

          unable to advance . . . . . unable to
                        return . . . . .

          some failure has damaged our
               élan . . . .

           an unfaithful friend

           failure in exams

           in work

        we no longer feel that blossoming dynamism

        we carry our bodies like lumps of lead,

           lumps of lead,

        we slumber into a world of disillusionment

          apathetic
          listless

but then comes change

      winter changes to spring

      we meet a friend

      we rest

    forces awaken in our bodies

    life seems to surge once more . . . .
                  as the morning sun

                  calm
                  unswerving
                  certain
                  never faltering

.........others fall,

        sink into sadness,

          rise

           but fall again too quickly......

            obstacle seems to follow obstacle

and they remain deflated....depressed....downhearted....

                      crushed

    life does not seem to blossom......

       the joy of living has fled

          maybe never was

from depression

       they are sucked into despair

from sadness

       into misery

....alone

the man in misery is crushed . . . . . encircled

without hope of rising by himself

surrounded and knotted with obstacles and
difficulties . . . . .

no desire

no hope

no motivation

no will to live

closed off

man is a marvelous and mysterious being

when called forth

calling forth

strength

tenderness

can surge up in him

giving life

and then there can be a bursting forth of quiet energy . . . . . .

capacity for creativity . . . . . . generosity . . . . . . deep

attention . . . . . . concern . . . . . . work . . . . . . a sense of

wonderment . . . . . . some taste of the infinite . . .

never ceasing . . . . evolving . . . . deepening . . .

creating . . . . . . calling . . . . . .

when something interests me
　　　　how easy it becomes
　　　　　　　　vital . . . . . living
no interest . . . . . apathy
　　　　　i wander down life's path
　　　　　　　　cynical
　　　　　and sad
　　　　　　　　　　sad unto death
　　　　how quickly i die
　　who will call me forth?

being down . . . . . . with no life

no beauty

that beauty which flows with life . . . . . .

eyes . . . .

living eyes . . .

not radiating

no longer a source of attraction . . . .

nothing in me attracts . . . .

people turn away their eyes . . . . .

i am not only dejected

but rejected

covered with shame

deserted . . . abandoned . . .

alone . . . . . in anguish

crucified

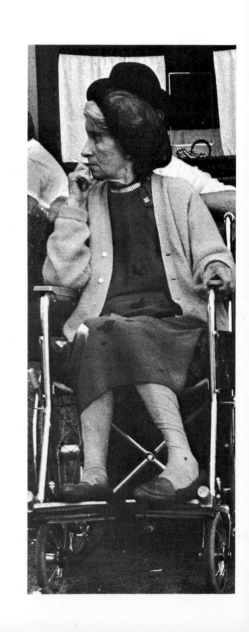

i who am dejected
      let go that inner hold......
           sink down......down.....
   friends drift downstream
               laughing....
i remain......lying on my bed
      smoking
      drinking
   or sitting....sitting
     the radio playing on and on and on
   waiting
   waiting
     but waiting for
       what.....

and i am afraid......

      those haggard eyes

         or open wounds

         or black skin or white skin

         or alcoholic smell

         or freaked out mind

            of the man in misery

      strike deep chords of fear within me....

fear of losing my money, time, reputation, liberty

    fear, above all, of losing myself

      fear of the unknown,

         for misery is a world of the unknown.....

      terror of despair,

         those hands.... those hands.....

         those hands stretched out towards
                         me....

         i am afraid to touch them......

          they may drag me down, down,

           down to some unknown
                    future........

i fear my helplessness
  my hollows
    my poverty

you remind me that i too must die

and so i turn my back
  returning to my home
    escaping the fundamental reality
      of my own existence,
        of my own poverty
          and yours, my brother.....
        i refuse to love......

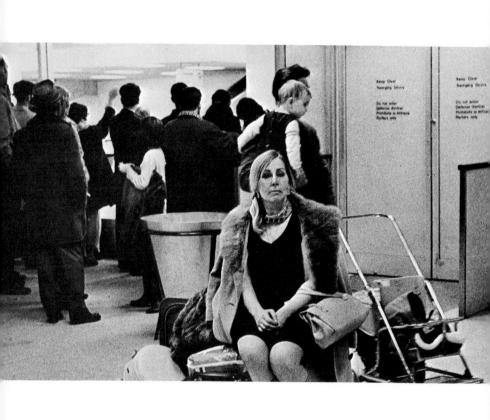

because i fear your grasping hand
                    calling me to the unknown
                        the unknown of love
because i fear my emptiness
                my poverty
                my call to death
            i fear myself
            i close my heart . . . . . cement block . . .
                    shut myself off
                    from you,
                            my despairing brother
you are in a prison of despair, sadness . . .
i too am in prison
    but my bars and locks
        are my so-called friends, clubs, social conventions,
            "what everybody else is doing" . . .
barriers that i have built
        that prevent me seeing you,
                my brother
your presence,
        miserable, sad . . .
            is a call . . . .
                do i turn away
                    or do i dare . . . . .
love is the greatest of all risks
        to give myself . . . . to you
            do i dare . . . . do i dare
                leap into the cool, swirling, living waters
                    of loving fidelity

.....the miserable man is still there
waiting...waiting....waiting for what
lying in his prison....
lying in his dung.....
waiting
yet
not waiting
for he has lost hope
we only wait when there is hope
where there is no hope......we lie.....dying
not living
sad unto death
yet he waits
waiting.............yet not waiting

the worthy lady, over rimmed glasses, saying:
    "lazy"
the bank manager shouting:
    "stupid"
are right. . . . in a way. . . .
the miserable man knows it only too well
his misery is the awareness of his misery
    "i remain in the vomit of my worthlessness. . . . ."

he knows this worthlessness
    and has lost hope
the man in misery is not ignorant
only lacking in strength. . . . vitality
that which springs from hope
        and he has no hope. . . . . .
his misery is greater because of his awareness
        therein lies his despair
        he cannot rise
        not feeling worthy to rise

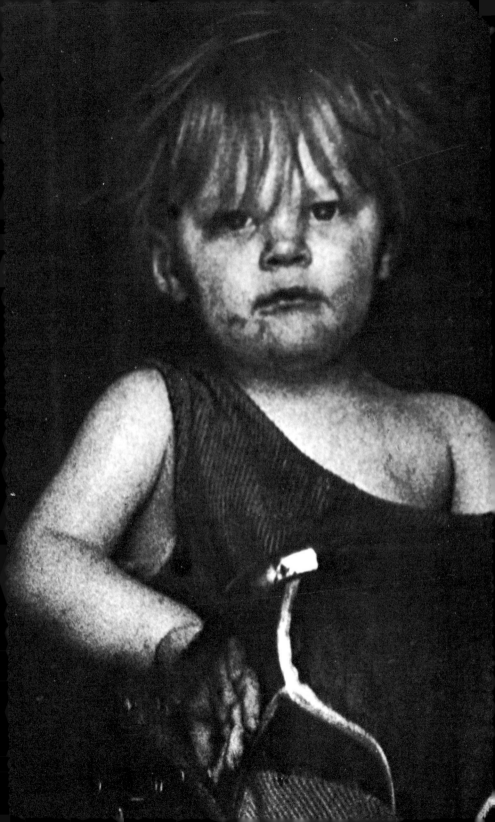

the person in misery does not need a look that
        judges and criticizes
     but a comforting presence
        that brings peace and hope and life
        and says:
            "you are a human person
                important
                mysterious
                infinitely precious
            what you have to say
                is important
                because it flows
                    from a human person
            in you there are those seeds
                    of the infinite
                    those germs of love...of beauty
                    which must rise from the earth
                                    of your misery
                    so humanity be fulfilled.
        if you do not rise
            then something will be missing
                if you are not fulfilled
                    it is terrible
                        you must rise again
                            on the third day.....
                rise again because we all need
                you
                for you are a child of God
                you, sam
                        john
                                willie mae
                    my brother....my sister
                        be loved
                        beloved"

In some mysterious way
      the quality of my presence my look
          brings to you life

        or death

that look......
      that hand......
            calls forth
                  life....hope....joy...

if
you believe in me
then maybe
i can do something worthwhile......
      maybe i am worthwhile
maybe i can do something with my life

thus
the light of hope begins to burn
   your constant trust in me
         communicates warm sensations of confidence
                  and faith

      that look in your eyes
            the touch of your hands
                  brings me some marvellous message of hope

"your slightest look easily will unclose me
though i have closed myself as fingers,
you open always petal by petal as Spring comes
(touching skilfully, mysteriously) her first
rose"
                              e. e. cummings

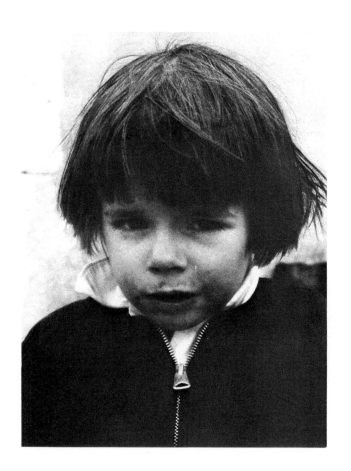

how then to approach the miserable child
　　　not haughtily
　　　　　　but humbly
　　　not judging but loving
　　　　　　determined not to dominate
　　　　　　not even to give things
　　　　　　rather to give myself
　　　　　　　　my time
　　　　　　　　　　energy
　　　　　　　　and heart

and to listen
　　　believing that he is important
　　　　　a child of God
　　　　　　　in whom Jesus lives

approach with tenderness
　　　　gently

gently giving one's friendship
　　　delicate soothing hands
　　　　bearing the oil of mercy
　　　　　annointing deep wounds

*"A new heart will I give you
and a new spirit I will put within
you and I will take out of your
flesh the heart of stone and give
you a heart of flesh."*
　　　　　　(ezechiel 36:26)

he who is

            or has been

                  deeply hurt

    has a RIGHT

        to be sure

          he is

         L O V E D

love!

      not just some passing moment

         a glance however open

but some deeper compassion

         radiating permanency

not some morbid curiosity

       some gushing pity

          incompetent naiveté

the cry of burnt-out eyes

         wounded bodies

      addicted minds

        cravings

can only be answered by some deeper love

      in which is felt a strange presence of the eternal

        a hope

        a new security

not some passing glance

       but deeper bonds

        unbreakable

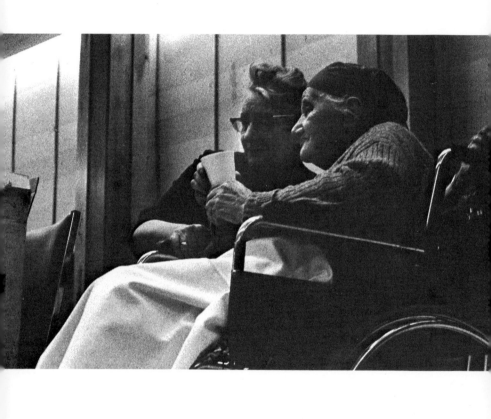

com-passion

     is a meaningful word.....
    sharing the same passion
      the same suffering
      the same agony
        accepting in my heart
          the misery in yours, o, my brother
          and you, accepting me

o yes there is fear
    but even more deeply
    there is the insistent cry from the entrails of the
                              suffering one
     that calls me forth.....

    some faint feeling
      of confidence
   that my smile......my presence
    has value and can give
      life

thus deep friendship is born
        mutual presence
        humble and forgiving
     engendering

         quiet joy
         fidelity

but

who will bring life to

the despairing,

to crushed and dying hearts

to those whose future is barred

to the mentally sick

to the aged and alone

to the despised and anguished

to the burnt out

statesmen are called upon to enact laws

but who is called to give hope to the despairing

how to approach him

he, repulsive and fearful

i, with my fear and my security

and yet......

i feel.....in some mysterious way

that there is a calling

the silent crying out of misery

tears of silence

and in my deepest being i hear this call

a sort of whispering

that life has meaning, but

in the degree that i find love

no reasons.....no reasons why......only a sort of.....

an act.....

an act of faith that i can enter into some vast and powerful

movement

of life and life giving

. . . . that my joy gives joy
my hope gives hope
and

that i can communicate in some silent way
the spirit living in me
not by what i say
but how i say it

a deep concern
a way of listening
to the faint heart beats
of your existence and life

listening
l i s t e n i n g
l i s t e n i n g
              whispering
              silent
              a listening that comforts
                  and calls forth

DO I DARE
do i dare
    believe
        your silent call
          your tears of silence

but there is the world of efficiency
              techniques
              diplomas
              business (and business is business!)

and then there are my friends
      who think i'm crazy.....are they friends?
                  am i crazy?

.......DOUBTS......

conflicting forces
        fatigue
        fears

and yet life calls forth
        compassion in my entrails

this strange and silent war
      do i dare
      do i dare
        believe
      do i dare
      do i dare

        surrender myself to your call

"if you pour yourself out for the hungry
          and satisfy the desire of the afflicted
                    then shall your light rise in the darkness
                         and your gloom be as the noonday
                              and the Lord will guide you continually

and you shall be like a watered garden
          like a spring of water
                    whose waters fail not."

                                        isaiah 58

o God
   my God
      keep me from flinching/waning
            slumbering into that timeless rest
            that never is
keep me from falling into a prison
                  of egotistical habits
                  where the bars
                  are superficial friends
                        and drinks
                        and stupid laughter
                        kisses without love
                        business and organisation
                        without heart
                        and gifts for self-flattery
               these bars that prevent life evolving
                     towards that taste of the infinite
                        open to your call. . . . .

break down those barriers
         that prevent me living, my God,
break down those barriers
         that threaten to stifle me. . . . . . .

barriers broken down too quickly
        are
            another form
              of death......
          too much exposure
          too much cold
    those who have learned life too quickly
      have thus lost life
   those who have thrown themselves into
               experiences of sexuality
             drugs for escape
        but who have lost life :
                  presence
                communion
         because love grows
            is a deepening fusion of peace
                  and liberty

i fear

the mysterious power of compassion

i

do not

believe in it

because that implies having found myself

that i no longer play

play a game

put on a mask — a personage

pretending to be

appearing

but that i become myself

accepting my poverty

letting the Spirit breathe

move
live
love

in me

opening my being
(no fear)

to the delicate touch

of His hand that opens me

but i fear

and wear my mask

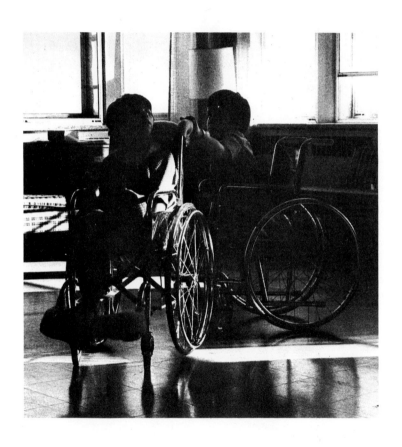

maturity of the heart:
        accepting
        myself
                with my limits
                in my poverty
                i do not fear
                        the
                        other

no fear that
                i will be eaten up
                devoured
                lose my being

no fear
            of showing who i am

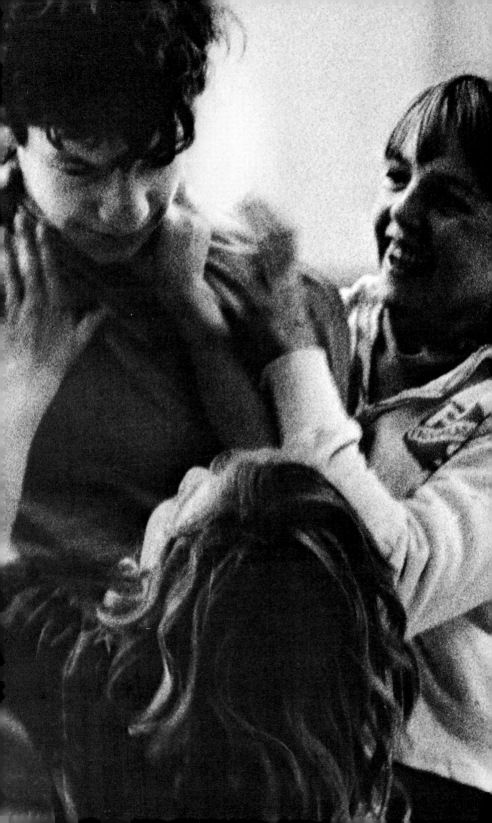

in each of us there is a need to

L I V E

the flowering out of life
the thirst for beautiful things

the feel of my radiance
                   in joy
                   in hope

in each of us there is a need to live
            but also

there are those seeds of death
                  no will to live
                  no desire to get up in the morning
                  never able to sleep. . . . always wanting
                                          to sleep. . . . .
                  but never sleeping

                  always down
                      and criticizing
                  no zest or energy
                  just-every-day-doing-what-i-must
                      with no zing
                          or laughter

i need to feel

        i am

       i am unique

          capable of love and life

             not just one of the crowd

                looking towards life

                  but myself living.....

i must not remain in a sort of

                    non-life

                    non-existence

                    closed in

                    despairing

       for this can be a taste of death........

life is a flowering vine.....
       too much light......or too little
       too much water......or too little
brings blight and death....burnt-up, dried up, drowned......

life needs delicate gentle hands, hands that know
just the right amount of water for life
just the right degree of light
at the right time....

or else, no life, no flower, no fruit.......

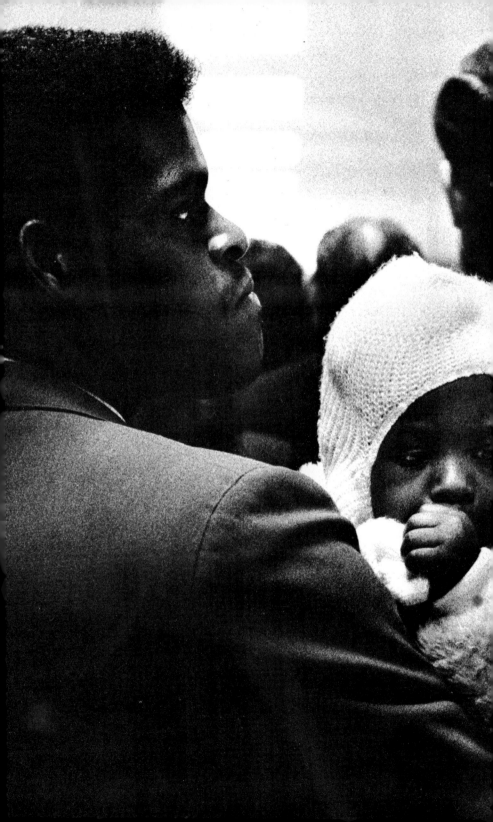

to evolve

        life does need security

            in the mother

            in the father

            in the home

                with friends

        but above all trust in the spirit

            against all assaults of fear and anguish

            against all the unknowns

            against anything that might destroy

                    the flowering of my life...

the biological movement
                    of growth
                        needs
this physical and spiritual
                        complement of love
                and so to evolve
                        the child
                        needs
                    the look
                    the hands
                        of his mother

life needs

                    security and hope

security being
the fundamental basis

                        the earth
                            in which life is born

hope being
that call . . . . . to light

                        and love
                          and beauty
                        . . . . . . universality
                        shadows of the infinite

risk
and hope
love of the unknown
passionate interest in the present

thirst for adventure
desire for new experiences

outpourings of generosity
quest for knowledge
openness to the future
call to love
availability to the Spirit
peaceful contemplation

high skies
mountains
deep lakes
deep breathing
wonderment

love is the greatest of all risks

the giving of myself

but do i dare take this risk
diving into the cool
swirling
living waters of

LOVING FIDELITY

an encounter
            is a strange
                        and wonderful thing
presence
one person to another
present
one to another
    life flowing
        one to another

but

we can be together
            and not meet

we can live in the same house day after day
            sit at the same table
            kneel at the same pew.
            read the same books
                but never meet

we can kiss
            gestures of love
            apparent tenderness
                but never meet

a meeting is a strange and wonderful thing

presence one person to another
            present one to another
            life flowing one to another

.......but to listen
                to listen intently
my God i wish i could listen
                        to my brother

listen to his heart beats

listen to those faint. . .o so faint. . .
                calls
                which are there
                hidden

under. . . . .i know not why. . . .
                some sort of fear

listening
                but instead
                i have my own ideas
                and i penetrate
                    destroying
                    harvesting all that is there

to make bread
                        for i
                        for me
                        for myself

i need to talk
   and walk
     with another

i need to express myself
   say things. . . . .

this is a movement of life
   life that is in me
     and needs to flow out. . . .

i must speak. . . . . and dance
   sharing things i love and hate
     my hopes, my joys, my fears, my griefs. . .
   giving myself
   giving my life
   giving life

a tiny child needs not only food and shelter
                    but something more...much more....
        a feeling of love
        that someone cares for him
                    ready to die for him
        that he is really loved
        that he is important....precious
            and so he begins to live
                    begins to sense the value of his being

and so it is that life rises in him
        and he grows in confidence
                        in himself
                    and in his possibilities of life
                            and of creation

effort

      conceived.....

          born...

             and nurtured

                in love

the miserable man   t
i treat you as a stranger. . . .   w
you were born and reared in   o
                    squalor. . .
you are walled in, for you have p
                 no life r
in front of you. . . . .no joys to i
                   look s
forward to. . . .no loving   o
             children. . . . n
no esteem   s

                    d
                    i
                    v   i, with my clean clothes, my
                    i   sensitive nose (i hate bad
                    d   smells)
                    e   my politeness. . . .a warm
                    d   house. . .
                 a world of security. . .the light
                of reality does not penetrate my
                  b   cell, the reality of human
                  y   misery
                so widespread, so deep. . . . .
                  a

                  g
                  u
                  l
                  f

two prisons divided by a gulf: the miserable
                      man. . . . . .
and, imprisoned in the cell next door, the man
                        of means
comfortably installed. . . . .and so the world
                      goes on,
and the gulf gets wider

       who will be the bridge

"i do not want to be reborn
   but if that should happen
      i would like to find myself amongst the untouchables
         in order to share their affliction,
                  their sufferings
               and the insults they are subject to.

in this way,
   perhaps i would have the chance
         to liberate them and myself
               from this miserable condition."

                              gandhi

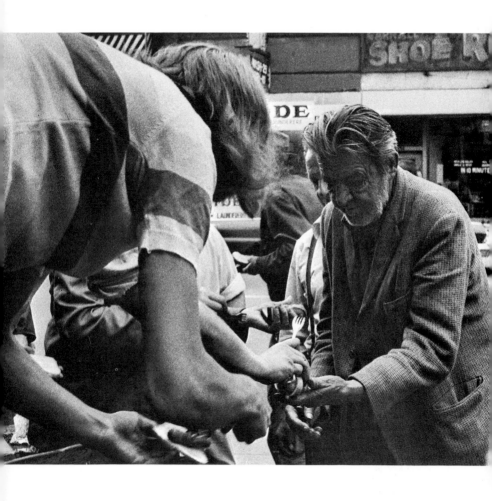

two worlds that never meet
       divided by a gulf called fear.....

who can assuage this fear

who can heal the wounds of this fear
            riches will not bring comfort
               to the man without hope....
          he needs the warm light of confidence
            a will to live....he knows his misery
              he is too convinced of his
                  apparent worthlessness
       what he lacks is not knowledge
        rather the hope and strength
          to rise from the filth.....

where to find this strength
      springing from hope
           which will conquer fear?

"blessed are the merciful

for they shall obtain mercy"

jesus

APPENDIX

Words addressed by M. Jean Vanier on Monday, January 3rd, 1972 at Church House, Westminster to an invited assembly after the showing of the Canadian film of the Pilgrimage at Easter, 1971, "FAITH AND LIGHT"

It was a fantastic experience, this reality of the Pilgrimage which in so many ways went much further than what we had planned or could ever have hoped for. I think the fundamental aspect that broke through was the real joy that was engendered and created by wounded people.

Living day by day, as I do, with men who have been called mentally retarded, men who have spent long years in psychiatric hospitals, or who have been doomed to inactivity, have been laughed at, stared at, I realise more than anything else that there is in them a feeling of their worthlessness, their poverty. I won't go into the whole psychology of handicapped people, But fundamentally, because they have heard so many people either pitying them or rejecting them, their hearts are often deeply wounded and they have this deep feeling that they are *no good*.

What is important for those who are called to live with or be close to handicapped people is not so much their technical knowledge, not so much even their professionalism—although it is obvious that we need doctors, psychologists, psychiatrists—the essential thing is that they may be able to look and to love and to welcome the handicapped person as a person, not so much because he is handicapped but because he is a person. This is the only thing that matters, because for so many years they have been carrying in themselves the fact that they have been termed mentally handicapped, mentally deficient, by people who think they are someone; by the so-called normal world which lives in its superiority and its grandeur. They (the handicapped) have been looked down on and rejected, put into asylums and homes which we know and visit. One of the big joys of this Pilgrimage was that over 500 men and women from Canada, from the U.S.A., from England and from France came from big institutions (psychiatric hospitals, subnormality hospitals and so on). Some of these men—one man had not been out of his particular hospital since 1916—were able to break down some of the barriers. With so many so-called normal people, the immediate reaction is, we know: fear, segregation, paternalism in the sense of "poor little children", and an incapacity to put their hands out and say "I welcome you, as you are with your slowness, your inability to speak, your difficulties, your crises, your epilepsy, your various problems".

The essential thing is to have people who just open their arms and accept the other person as he is. When he feels that he is accepted, he begins to realise that he is loved, not by some sort of pity, some sort of feeling that "I must do something for you", but because he is a person; then gradually barriers break down. Yet, this wounded person, when he is rejected, looked down on, feared and so on would sink into a world of sadness or else occasionally turn to violence, which is very natural. Any of us who have suffered from anguish through rejection, know full well that we get angry and that we could even get violent. If one can only break down these barriers of ours, our problems, our fears . . . . because the problems of mentally handicapped people are not so much mentally handicapped people themselves, but the so-called normal world that has rejected them and put them into big institutions. This is the problem. We have constructed a society that rejects the weak. This is a terrible indictment of any society. It is a wonderful thing when you put your arms out in a welcoming attitude to a handicapped person; then something happens: his eyes begin to believe and his heart begins to dance and he begins in some way to become our teacher. I think any of our assistants working in our homes would be able to say that we do nothing or very little; we can teach little but we are taught a lot.

We are taught a lot in realms where possibly we didn't expect to be taught; for it is true that when some people come to help in our homes, they come because they feel they might be able to do something or they want to do good. Gradually they begin to see—perhaps a smile that opens up and begins to touch me in the depths of my being. I begin to discover something: that this wounded person, a distorted face, a crippled hand, that the way the handicapped person looks at me, approaches me—all this does something to me, the wounded person calls me forth. And being called forth, I discover that I can bring him up some tiny little way. One of our assistants said to a group that she had been completely bowled over when she saw one of our men smile. This man had come recently from a psychiatric hospital, he was crushed and fearful; he is 25, has no family and had spent most of his life in the psychiatric hospital. She saw his first smile after he had been with us several weeks. She discovered that she could give life, just by her presence, by her constant tenderness, by her gentleness, by her weakness, by at the same time constant vigilance. She found she could bring this "child" to life; that her presence, her look, could bring him forth and she made the fantastic discovery that we are brought to life by the eyes and hands and call of wounded people who seem to call us forth to life.

One of the most fantastic things that happened on this Pilgrimage was that over a thousand young people came to help us. There were between four and five thousand handicapped people and some thousand young people between the ages of 16 and 25 who discovered something. Until then they had been doing things, possibly transforming matter, possibly learning great and wise things from books, but they had not discovered what is the greatest thing in a human person: this capacity to give life and to give life by calling handicapped people forth, and they responding and beginning to rise. It is a wonderful thing to see wounded people beginning to smile, be they handicapped, be they old, be they people in hospitals—people, lonely people throughout the world—and if you approach them tenderly and quietly and they begin to realise that somebody cares, that somebody is interested in them, then the eyes of death which were theirs, begin gradually to open and become eyes of life and of love. And these eyes of life and of love which in some strange way I have created, but not I—the Spirit of God living in me—these eyes waken and call me forth even more.

So gradually we enter into a world of communion and of sharing. We have now had quite a lot of experience of these little communities with handicapped people. For instance, in the village I am returning to tonight, we have 120 handicapped men and women living in small homes of ten or twelve; living with them are about 80 assistants. In Canada we have another home, and I have just returned from India after visiting the two homes, one at Bangalore and the other in the south at Kotagiri. Wherever we are there seems to be the same reality of wounded people taken from psychiatric hospitals calling forth the assistants and the assistants calling them forth and creating a community of peace and of joy.

I would say that over the years whilst I have had the joy to be present to handicapped people, they have taught me a number of things: Be simple, don't try to pretend that we are other than we are; learn to laugh and to sing and to dance and remember that a life that is led in a sad way is not worth living. Let us come down from the pedestals of our grandeur and come and enjoy life with other people in a simplicity of communion, in a simplicity of laughter. I have found that the most important thing for an educator, a person who calls himself an educator or a person who is called to live with handicapped people, is to learn how to laugh, because laughter and joy are the first signs of education and the first reality that groups people together: to grow together.

I feel very moved particularly by the amazing call of the hearts of wounded people to life in the Spirit, to understand—but no, not to understand—to *live* a Christian life. I would say that they have taught me because they have brought me down from the books of theology and philosophy into which I had sometime delved, to a reality which is the living of life. They can talk so simply of love. In our homes we gather together at night to pray together. Be it in Bangalore where nine Hindu men live with us or in France or Canada. In Bangalore we may spend half an hour in the morning and another half hour at night praying together; they sing in their language, which is not our language, and we sing with them in our language. Then Shrinivasan and Gurunathan and others pray in their very simple way, as the candle flickers they talk about God, how God loves them, how God has brought us peace and how they themselves are called to enter into a world of love. Or sometimes, equally simply, they say that today they had a "bagarre" and fought with someone and that they are sorry, and that they know God will forgive them. When I listen to them I am always very moved because they are in many ways our masters. The books of theology, however necessary they may be and all the wisdom of the world are very little, compared to simple people with their gestures of affection and of kindness for in their simple words of prayer, they can teach us, just by what they are, that this world can become a land of love.

Handicapped people and all those who have occasion to come close to them, could be the salvation of mankind if those who are on the pedestals of normality, leave these pedestals, become people, not people who think they are normal with respect to abnormaility, but just *people*. We are all handicapped, we are all handicapped—we know it. We are all carrying the weight of our self-centredness, our fears, our incapacity to communicate, our difficulties in generosity and in communion, we have this equally in us; we are all deeply handicapped. If we could only realise that these are not the normal and the abnormal but just people going along at different speeds; their hearts moving at different speeds; but they are all people! And if only those who think they are normal, at least those who have intelligence and force and capacity, could unite, create homes, and schools and leisure for those who are wounded! For these wounded people are there: as you know in practically every county there is a large subnormality hospital and sometimes two or three.

The Government White paper concerning mental retardation, mental handicap, gives the numbers of mentally handicapped people for whom they are hoping within the next few years small homes will be established. The work is there; the wounded are there; but the terrible thing is that the helpers are not there and yet a great work should be done and can be done if we accept one thing: to share our lives with them. We are not there particularly to do good to them. They don't want people to do good to them but to share it; to eat with them; to laugh with them; to pray with them; as brothers and sisters; to enjoy leisure with them; to dance with them; to celebrate with them. We must find the way to encourage people to do this, with seriousness, with devotion, with perseverance and also with real knowledge. In this way, those who leave their pedestals will be re-created and they will discover some of the real meaning of life and of love and they will be reborn. I think that those who have really lived with handi-capped people have been reborn in their hearts because they have learnt to drop the barriers. They have learnt to drop the barriers and to look at people, to laugh with them; and to say without shame or without fear or without complexes: I love you and I know that you love me and in our communion together, in our compassion, mutual compassion we can celebrate life together. And possibly, together, you and I (you with your more exterior handicap and I with all my interior handicaps), we can give to this world some touch of joy, for this is what our world is looking for, this is what our world is thirsting for: JOY. I think that in the degree that we open our hearts to the handicapped, we gather joy. If we let the barriers drop, if we accept the sufferings of our days, we will gradually enter into a world of peace and of joy and we know that where love is, God is too. And frequently we meet Jesus Christ and the presence of God in the wounded people who are rising up.